Cameras for Kids, Fun And Inexpensive Proje

Hello and thank you for taking a peek at Camera created for kids that can read at approximately a **4**th grade level, but age may vary depending on the child's reading and comprehension ability. I recommend all parents to take a look through the book before allowing their child to start on the projects or reading the book. Parents should use their own discretion as far as their child's ability to do these projects safely. I have made every effort to make these projects fun, safe, and inexpensive. This book will hopefully serve as a guide to photography and artistic expression for the little photographer / artist. If you have any thoughts or concerns about any of these projects, you may want to accompany your child while doing the project or skip one that you do not feel comfortable with.

Teachers, this book may be a great way to teach the basics of photography to younger kids. If buying a bunch of cameras is not an option for your school, you might want to print out enough photos for each child in the class, then do some of the projects out of the book without the expense of all the extra gear. I've tried to make this book easily adaptable to a school environment as well as a home setting. Visit - www.camerasforkids.info - for more information.

All text and images in this book are © John Crippen, **2009**. If you have any questions about this book or the use of any of it's content, you can reach me through my website at www.photo-scenix.com or by email at... JohnCrippenPhotography@gmail.com I often license images to books, magazines, papers, and other publishing mediums as well.

TABLE OF CONTENTS

The stars next to each section of the book represent an approximate level of difficulty. 1 star being 7 years and up, 2 stars being 10 years and up, and 3 stars are for 13 years and above. The star system is by no means an absolute, but a good barometer for the difficulty of the projects.

INTRODUCTION TO THE BASICS

CAMERA SHOOTING PROJECTS

ARTS AND CRAFTS WITH YOUR PHOTOS

Supplies List

Most of the supplies needed for these projects were bought from a local dollar store, with the exception of the camera. (we'll get to the camera later) Note that the supplies that I picked are often examples and that you don't have to buy the same exact items that I have.

Rubber Animals, $1.00 each. I chose a Rhino and a Hippo

Tape, I got two rolls of clear tape for $1.00

Tape, masking type, I got a roll of blue masking tape for $1.00

Crayons, I got a set of 64 colors in a nice plastic case for $1.00

Black, fine tip permanent markers, a four-pack for $1.00

2 Poster Boards 22"x28", one white and the other in color, both for $1.00

Miniature Tripod, a great deal at only $1.00, they're pretty universal, too

2 small clip-on lights with batteries included, $1.00 each.

36 Sheets of 12"x19" construction paper in assorted colors for $1.00

3-Pack of beveled pre-cut matting for 4"x6" prints, $1.00 for the set

1 Pair of scissors for $1.00 and a pair of jagged edged scissors $1.00

1 Photo Album for 4"x6" prints, and another for 8"x10" prints, $1.00 each

1 - 8 oz. bottle of glue $1.00

A bunch of cool stickers, $1.00 for the whole set

So for a grand total of $18.00 plus taxes, you have the basic supplies to do the projects in this book. This does not include the expense of buying a camera, or the required accessories for the camera.

Most of the items used for these projects can be found in places such as your local dollar store, but supplies are different in every location. From time to time I will try to offer alternative or substitute supplies to compensate for the variance among different shopping areas. The idea was to give parents an almost unlimited resource of inexpensive tools and materials for their kids. Above all else, have fun with this book and try to actively participate with you child to make this a wonderful memory while stimulating an important part of the growth and development process.

The rubber critters can be just about anything the imagination calls for. It can be other objects that kids are interested in as well. Buildings, cars, trees, or any kind of inexpensive toys that can be used with these projects.

One of the main things to note is that these objects do not have to be very big. The idea is for the child to learn perspective and space by using camera angles to create the impression of a giant beast or object. These toys will also help develope story telling imagination.

Two different types of tape are going to be used in this book. The clear tape for times when you want to tape from the front and not be visible. The masking tape will come in handy when taping objects and surfaces such as walls and other spots where you want the tape to peel off easily

Crayons will come in handy for all kinds of projects and are great ways to teach kids about colors, shapes, and forms. This particular set came with 64 colors in a nice solid plastic box.

The markers came four in a pack. Bare in mind that these markers say PERMANANT for a very good reason. The markers can be used for all kinds of projects and can be used in conjunction with the crayons. Depending on your childs age and other factors, you may want to keep a close eye on them while using the markers. As a matter of fact, that may be a good idea with all the materials and devices expressed in this book.

The poster board above came 2 for
a dollar. They are both 22"x28", so
they are a lot larger than they look in
the book. When you pick them up,
try to find one in white, and the other
in any color your child would like.

The mini-tripod may come in handy
for a few projects, but the main reason
for the tripod is for creating an
"Infinity Wall". More an that subject
later in this book.

The item on the bottom is a mini
clip on light. It's small, compact,
and clips onto other objects. The
batteries came with it. Not bad for
a dollar! I recommend buying more
than one of these lights if you find them.
Often times, you'll need more than one
angle of light to get a great shot.

This multiple colored construction paper came in 36 - 12"x19" pages. Construction paper can be used for many purposes other than the projects in this book. Kids love colors and the possibilities with this paper are endless, stock up on it!

The scissors will be used to create some of the projects in this books, especially projects involving the construction paper. Use caution while allowing you child to use scissors. Kids will run, jump, poke and peek at or around almost anything. although curiousity is a healthy part of developement, it can also get somebody hurt. If you have any doubts with any items or tasks in this book, use your better judgement. At the very least, have an adult accompany them.

The item on the left is a 3-pack of pre-cut matting made to fit 4"x6" photo prints. Not only can the kids mat their photos in these, the matting will also be used later in this book to help teach photo composition and teach kids how to "frame" their shots. At three for a dollar, these little mats are a great deal.

The item on the left is a small photo album used to hold 4"x6" photos. These little photo albums can be used with the construction paper and scissors to make creative mini scrapbooks as well. Along with the projects in this book, there will be plenty of materials left to think outside the box and create your own projects for kids. There's plenty of items I didn't pick up at the local dollar store that would be great for scrapbooking. Paste, string, ribbon, confetti, labels, colored markers, ink pens, stickers, and much more. Most dollar stores have an aisle full of goodies for just such a project. Many big box stores, stationary stores, and school supply stores are helpfull as well.

This photo album fits 8"x10" photos. It's got a lot of nice trim and would be another good album for scrapbooking. One thing about most of the places such as dollar stores, they change their inventory frequently. If you see something you really like, you may want to stock up on it. These larger albums are also perfect for parents, a refridgerator can only hold so many pictures and magnets. Even though they change photos albums often, there always seems to be something nice to choose from. Hobby shops can be pricey, but sometimes will have fantastic sales comparable to the dollar stores. The same thing holds true for the big box stores as well.

Here's a few last minute items for the scrapbooking part of the projects...

The squiggly scissors will be fun for cutting out interesting shapes with the prints and construction paper and, were a great deal at a buck!

The stickers can be used for a bunch of the crafts portion of the book. $1.00 a set.

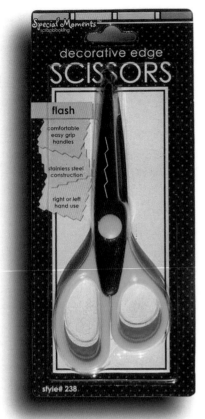

Usually the dollar stores have some kind of paste, but I did my shopping right after the back to school rush. I did manage to find an 8 ounce tube of glue for $1.00. Hopefully you'll be able to find the paste as the glue can be a little harder to use while keeping the area clean. If you can't find glue or paste, you can always try the tape.

Camera Selection For Young Photographers

For the most part, you just want to keep the selection simple. A point and shoot from a good camera brand. Look for a sturdy housing and a flash that does not pop up. The pop-up flashes tend to get broken easily by smaller kids. Some point and shoots are now water resistant, too. another good idea for young kids that drop or spill.

Try to find a camera with a good size monitor on the back. Buttons and controls should be simple and easily accessable. Try to find a camera with the most standardized needs. Compact Flash (CF) and Secure Digital (SD) RAM are the most common types of memory cards for digital cameras. You'll get more memory for less money this way.

For kids, I recommend getting a camera that uses standard AA or AAA type batteries. Preferrably rechargables. Kids tend to do a lot of shooting. When going on trips, kids may run out of batteries or forget them altogether, so having standard battery capability is great while on the go!

Other Considerations While Picking Out A Camera

A Preset Dial on the outside of the camera is a very helpful function. Rather than having to learn complex concepts such as Aperture, ISO, Shutter Speed, and Exposure settings, kids can just turn the dial to the picture. Some cameras make you go through a menu system within the camera, but if you can find a camera with the external dial for these functions, it will be a lot easier to learn.

Image Stabilization is another nice function to have. Sometimes referred to as IS, VR, or other name, this function uses a motor on the lens to help keep the camera steady while taking a shot. This function is especially important with fast moving objects or working in low light situations. Image Stabilization has become fairly common on newer point and shoots.

Camera's you may want to avoid... Some cameras are very propriatary and will only allow you to use their own brand of accessories, batteries, and / or memory cards. Generally speaking, I would avoid these cameras for kids. Children will drop things, toss things, and misplace things. Propriatary items are usually more expensive and harder to find. The last thing you want to do on a road trip is spend four hours looking for that 'special' battery. If you get on line and research cameras before buying, you will probably catch on real quick on which brands to avoid.

Camera accessories are important, but can add up pretty quick. Things that you'll need for a good day of shooting include a couple extra memory cards, a couple sets of extra batteries, a car & house charger for the batteries, a camera cleaning cloth, an inexpensive tripod, and a nice carrying case that will protect the camera from impact. Make sure the case has enough room for the charger, camera manual, and other extras mentioned above. Child Safety, you may or may not want a strap on the camera or the camera bag. Kids can easily get snagged or caught up on an object or vehicle. This is a matter you'll have to use some discretion on. You don't want to buy another camera, but safety first.

Basic Camera Functions

 BACKLIGHT, when the sun is shining at the camera, this puts out a little bit of flash. The camera is trying to balance the light.

 Battery life meter, this symbol means the battery is full

 Battery life meter, this symbol means the battery is half full

 Battery life meter, this symbol means the battery is empty

 Beeper (two different symbols) this turns beeper on / off

 Garbage Bin or Delete Button, this button is used to remove pictures you don't want. It will usually ask "Are you sure?" before deleting the picture

 This symbol means the flash is on

 This symbol means the flash is turned off

 This button will lock pictures so they cannot be accidently erased. The same button can also unlock pictures to erase

 The Redeye function, when this function is turned on, the camera strobes the flash so you don't get the "Devil Eyes"

 Self timer mode, this will turn on the timer so you can be in the picture with you family or friends. Don't forget to use a tripod when using the camera's timer.

Camera Modes For Getting That Perfect Shot

  Landscape mode will try to make everything in focus. It will also brighten the blues & greens. Best used for mountains, trees, and nature.

 Macro mode is best used for closeups of flowers, insects, and small creatures like lizards. You have to be very still with this mode, so you might want to use a tripod. Macro mode will try to focus only on the main part of the picture.

 Night mode is used for shooting people and items in low light situations. When in night mode, you will still need a little light for it to work properly. The camera will be using a slow shutter speed, so use a tripod while in this mode.

 Portrait mode is used for taking pictures of people in good lighting conditions. It will try to keep the person in focus while bluring or (softening) the background. The camera will try to get some nice skin tones, too.

 Sport mode will try to track fast moving objects. This mode is good for catching people, pets, or cars while moving. Sport mode usually does not like to use the flash, so you will have to use this in good daylight.

Introduce children to the camera by having it with you and occasionally taking a snap of them doing things. You can also take funny pictures of pets or pretty pictures in nature. Get them used to being around the camera and understanding what it's for. Gradually allow them to take pictures once in a while, but under your guidance. Emphasize that a camera is an expensive device and that they need to be very careful while handling it. Let them know it's OK to run around and play in front of the camera, but that they must be still while using the camera. You can also demonstrate the difference in behavior while shooting, rather than playing in front of the camera. Kids learn through practice. After your child is used to taking snaps, begin to teach them about different lighting conditions and how this effects the pictures. Gradually introduce other scenarios such as movement, different distances, and times of day.

Once they are familiar with the camera and how to use it safely, you can start to teach them about some of the presets in the camera. Introduce them to the different modes such as the landscape mode, macro mode, night shot mode, portrait mode, and sport mode. Give them a little time to experiment in each of the preset modes so they get an understanding of what each mode is good for. Practice using the different modes with them, too. The presets in the camera often serve more than one type of situation. The only way to find out the full capabilities of each mode is to spend a little time with each one. You'll be amazed how fast kids learn and what beautiful pictures they'll be taking in no time. After you and your child are comfortable using the camera and have an understanding of all the presets, it's time to learn some basic rules of composition. Expect the unexpected and be aware it's not unusual for the camera to get dropped a couple times.

Basic Rules of Composition

Basic rules of composition are more of a guideline than something set in stone. There's always exceptions to the rule, and many well known photographers will break these rules from time to time and "think outside the box." They are however a good rule of thumb in most situations. One of the most basic rules is called the Rule of Thirds. Simply put, the main subject of the picture should be slightly to one side or the other, not exactly in the middle. The Rule of Thirds can be applied from right to left, or from top to bottom. Below is a couple different examples of this rule.

Notice how the girl's eyes in this picture line up with the upper third of the image. The eyes are often a point of referrence when gaging the Rule of Thirds. If her eyes were in the center of the photo, it probably wouldn't be as appealing. This photo also tells a story, another idea for good composition.

The photo below uses the Rule of Thirds in an up and down manner. You can also use this rule from side to side as well. Setting up activities for kids to do is a fun way to get good shots. Kids do not tend to have those awkward poses if they're busy having fun.

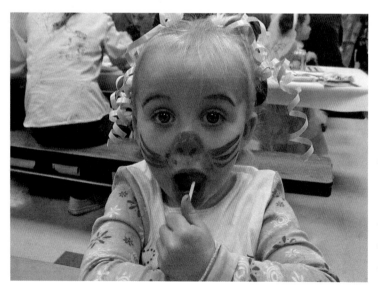

The girl on the top was in the middle of creating a news paper. The girl on the bottom had her face painted for halloween and is enjoying her halloween candy. Special occassions and holidays are a perfect time for kids to practice on each other. When they get tired of shooting, you can run the AV cable into the TV and have a slideshow!

Backgrounds can be good or bad, depending on your surroundings, and what kind of story you're trying to tell. Sometimes the background is important because it has specific elements to your story, but other times it just creates distractions... This picture was taken in a zoo, if you shoot from

too far back, you'll be catching the fences, walls, feeders, and other things that would distract the eye away from the bright colors of the Flamingo. Also, details in shades of pink are hard to catch from a distance. By closing in on the bird, you can see every feather and the sharp details of his eye.

Notice how the background compliments the Salamander in this one. The small twigs and brush tell you how small this little guy is. Nice contrast, too!

Angles can have a huge effect on your pictures, too. You can take a boring subject and make it look amazing just by changing the way you look at it. A simple piece of cheese can become interesting by using cool angles.

After shooting an object straight on, try shooting it from the left, then again on the right. After changing you horizontal angle, trying the same thing with your vertical angles... Shoot the object from above, then try again from a lower point of view. Sometimes a simple shift in position can tell a whole new story. A fun way to try this is by shooting small objects in macro mode. Flowers, toys, foods, and many other small objects are perfect for this. Some photographers make a living just doing this type of shooting.

Another thing to try is placing small objects together in various places and arrangements. Imagine the block of cheese above with a couple olives and some kind of garnish. Sometimes the smallest details make the biggest improvements in a picture. They can help complete the story. Try looking through the advertisements in a magazine and you'll see all kinds of ideas for angles, arrangements, and small details.

Lighting is important to any photograph. Without light, you cannot have a photograph. (at least a little light anyways) Even the slightest change in light can make a big difference on how your photos will turn out. Portraits are a good example of how a little light can make a big difference. Have you ever heard the old saying "chin up and shoulders back"? Lighting is one of the reasons for that saying. The shoulders back raises the head and the chin up helps prevent unwanted shadows. In the case of most portraits, you want to keep the skin tones as even as possible. Sometimes photographers take portraits in a low light environments. That's why some portrait photographers have so many lights pointing at the person in all kinds of different angles. They're trying to eliminate unwanted shadows.

This was a tough shot to get the light just right. If I had used a flash in the shot it would have bounced off the mirror and ruined the photo. The light in the hotel was not too bright. Cameras shoot slower in low light, so there's more chance of having unwanted blur or loss of sharpness. When cameras are shooting in low light, try to use a tripod. This will help eliminate "camera shake", the dreaded side effect of slower shutter speeds. This is how the camera adjusts itself to low light, it keeps the shutter open a little bit longer to catch the right amount of light.

When shooting, try to shoot the same shot in both horizontal and vertical. You might just be surprised. The switch from one format to the other will change lighting and color as well as the shape of the photo. This also gives you more options while framing or mounting them, too.

Horizontal is (Landscape)

Vertical is (Portrait)

VERTICAL

HORIZONTAL

A few last minute tips before we start on the projects...

If you're not sure if you have enough light, use a tripod, try with and without using the flash and decide which way you like better afterwards.

If you need help figuring out how you want to shoot something, try making a picture frame with your fingers. Look at the shot through your "Frame".

If you're background is too bright, trying holding your sunglasses over the lens. This is called Polarizing, and will sometimes help balance out lighting.

When shooting portraits, make the person feel more comfortable by talking with them. Find out what kinds of things they like to do for fun. When people talk about things they enjoy, they naturally light up.

Try to keep an extra set of batteries and an extra memory card with you whenever you go out to shoot. You may go out to shoot one thing, and discover something else really cool while you're there.

When you're playing around with different angles, don't be afraid to get creative. Lay on your back and shoot straight up at a tree, turn sideways to shoot a car, try shooting something from far away and then up close, try using the Rule of Thirds, then try breaking the rules!

Try shooting with a friend and exchanging roles. Sometimes be the photographer, then sometimes be the model. Share your ideas with each other. Sometimes you can learn more by being in front of the camera than behind it.

Shoot the same thing in different camera modes.... Portrait, Landscape, Macro, Nightshot, Sports Mode, or any other options your camera has. Take a look through the photos afterwards. What changed? Which one did you like the best for that type of shot? Why?

Practice practice practice!

Making An Infinity Wall

First off, what is an infinity wall? An infinity wall is a simple way to change lighting and shadows on small objects without having to spend a lot of money. It can be used to eliminate unwanted shadows, or enhance shadows making a more dramatic scene. This technique is often used by photographers that shoot food, jewelry, toys, or small collectable items.

Items needed for this project... a white 22'x28" poster board, some masking tape, a couple mini clip-on lights, a miniature tripod, and a small item to shoot with your camera. I used the plastic hippo for this experiment.

Tape the top of the poster board to a wall or other surface that the tape will stick to without harming anything. Do this length ways from the top down (vertical format).

About half of the paper should be on the wall, and the other half on the floor. Once you have a smooth curve in the paper, tape the other end down to the floor. The idea here is to eliminate the sharp corner between the wall and the floor. Masking tape is pretty easy to work with. If you have to adjust the position of the poster board, don't worry if you have to change things around a little, the tape will stick. Clip one of the lights on each side.

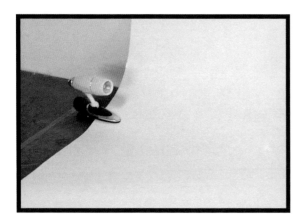

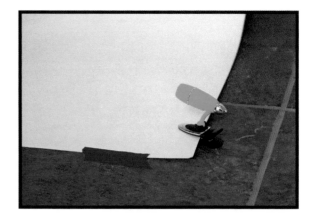

Position the tripod in front of the infinity wall. Spread the legs out as far as possible to make sure your camera will be steady. Carefully set the camera on the tripod. The easiest way to do this is to turn the camera up side down, and screw the tripod into the camera. Double check all the screws and adjustments on the tripod before setting it down. The camera should be steady on the legs of the tripod before you let go of it. Now make any slight adjustments to make sure the camera is pointing at your object and is focusing properly. Take a couple sample shots to be sure.

Here's a basic setup for an infinity wall. The poster board is evenly spaced between the wall and the floor, there's a light on each side, and the tripod holding the camera is placed directly in front of the poster board. Notice how the object (Hippo) is right in the middle of the paper. This is pretty much the only thing that should always be the same... The object should always be centered.The camera and lights can be moved around though.

Now that you have an idea of how to set up the infinity wall, it's time to experiment. Move the clip-on lights around on the poster board. In front and behind of the object as well as above and below the object. You can even put both of the lights on the same side of the poster board to create long dramatic shadows. Making these huge shadows will make the object appear bigger. You can also use the lights in your house to do some of the work,

Congratulations, you've just completed the hardest project in the book! I wanted to start here because lighting is the most important element of mastering photography. Now that you've made the infinity wall and have an understanding of it, try to master the shadows and lighting. Move the camera around, move the lights around, and see if you can hide all the shadows while lighting up your object. Stretch the shadows and shrink the shadows until you think you've got the lighting techniques figured out. Now try doing this with all the different camera modes... Portrait, Macro, Landscape, and so on. Try doing these techniques with the flash on, and with the flash off. If your flash is a little too bright, try putting a thin piece of tissue over the flash, this will diffuse or muffle the flash and make the lighting less harsh. A piece of Kleenex may work well for this.

Sharpness... Sometimes it's hard to get the focus just right while using an infinity wall. Try moving the camera back a little bit or changing the angle the camera is hitting the object at. You may need more light or a different camera mode. Don't forget to move the clip-on lights around again, too.

Making Critters and Toys Glow! Now that you know how to make an infinity wall, try making one in color this time. I like blue for doing the glowing effects because there's lots of contrast with the lighting. This time I didn't attach the lights to the poster board. I just put the Rhino in the middle of the blue infinity wall and setup the camera on the tripod. To make objects glow, you need to set this up in a dark place. (that is, after you set up, turn out the lights)

The camera needs to be set on night mode with no flash. This will make the shutter speed slower. Ideally you want at least a 2 or 3 second shutter. In other words, from the time you click the shot, it should take 2 or 3 seconds before the camera is done snapping that one shot.

Right after you click the shoot button on the camera, take out the little clip-on light or a flashlight and circle around the object. (but not directly on the object) keep circling around and around until the camera is done taking the shot. In the pictures above, you can see the difference with and without the light.

The glowing effect can also be done on large objects and friends. It's a great way to make pictures for Halloween, too. You can make pumpkins or gouls glow in the dark by using this trick. Remember to use the tripod and have them stand still for best results. When ever you're using a slow shutter speed, there's a lot better chance of a picture coming out blurry. Speaking of gouls, you can use the slow shutter speed trick to turn your friends into a ghost!

Set the camera on a slow shutter speed by putting it in night shot mode. Have the camera on a tripod. Have your favorite ghost or goul standing in front of the camera when you snap the shot. After about 1 second, have them step backwards out of the shot. The shutter should still be open for about another second or two. When you look back at the photo, the person should look like a ghost. (see through) Timing this shot isn't always easy and can take a lot of practice. Once you have got it just right a couple of times, it becomes really easy! You'll get a sense of the shutter timing and be able to time it well.

Shutter Priority is an advanced function some cameras have. Turn the dial to the - S - and you can now make the shutter as fast or slow as you would like. These camera's will have a dial to turn the shutter speed up and down. by doing this, you control exactly how much light goes into the camera. Cool huh? If your camera has this, you can time things easier.

A little bit about zooming in and out... (No, not a race car!) The lens on a camera has the ability to change it's focal length. Simply put, it has the ability to make things look closer or further from you while you're taking a picture. Zooming in causes things to look closer to the camera, while zooming out makes things look further from the camera. Most camera's have a switch marked with a T (for Telephoto) and W (for Wide Angle). When you press down on the T everything gradually starts getting closer and closer. When you press down on the W everything gradually moves further away from you. The camera's lens works very much like your own eye. That's why you can read a book a few inches in front of you, then look up at a bird way up in a tree. The eyes are much faster than a camera's lens, but kind of work the same way.

The photo on the left was taken while the camera was zoomed all the way in. I held down the T until it wouldn't zoom in any closer. The photo on the right was taken while the camera was zoomed all the way out. I held down the W until the camera couldn't get any futher back. Note that I never actually moved. I was standing in the same place for both shots, I just used the zooming in and zooming out feature on the camera to create a different Focal Length.

The switch for this function is usually on the front of the camera, or on the top of the camera (but near the front). It's usually pretty close to the button that snaps the picture. In the diagram on the left you can see the W and the T on the top of the camera.

Right now let's try zooming all the way out. Hold down the **W** and you'll be gradually backing out (moving further away) from the object.Once the camera won't back out any further, you are in full Wide Angle mode. When a camera is in wide angle mode, it can sometimes have a really cool effect on what ever you're shooting. It can make things look far away, but it can also make things look really big, or really small by changing the angle of your shot.

This is obviously a little girl, but by backing out the zoom and crouching down really low, she looks like a giant! This is why zooming out is often referred to as Wide Angle. It can make things look really big, tall, or wide. Something else can be fun about the wide angle function. look at the background. See how distorted it is. Everything on the left looks like it's leaning over to the right. Everything on the right looks like it's leaning over to the left. Depending on how you want your background to look, this could be good, or this could be bad. In this case, since the little girl is the main object in the picture, it's kind of a cool effect.

This picture tells a story about two girl's friendship. In this shot I was lying on the leaves under the trees and trying to make them look as tall as possible. Sometimes you can get 4 or 5 people to stand in a circle and get a really fun shot using this technique. The trees above them not only added to the picture, but blocked the direct sunlight as well.

OK, While we're on the subject of making objects look huge, let's try it out on the rubber critters. For this shot it's fun to have some background in the picture to make it look like the animals are wondering through some Brush. Your lawn is a perfect example for this. If you don't have a lawn, take your camera and critters with you the next time you go to the park. Place the object in the middle of some grass or brush, then crouch down low. The idea is to make it look like you're looking up at a giant beast! Take a couple shots and check to make sure you are getting proper focus. If the critters appear blurry, the auto focus had something between the object and the camera. It may be focusing on a blade of grass instead of the object. Another reason a camera may not focus correctly is because you are too close to the object and the camera cannot focus on the object. Cameras have limits on how close or how far you can be from the object. Once you've mastered this shot, move things around a little and even turn the critter around in different poses. Change your camera angles, too. Another trick with critters is to leave more space on the side of the picture that the animal is facing.

Remember the Rule of Thirds? In this picture, leaving a little extra space in the direction the animal is facing makes you wonder where he is going. It makes it look like he is going somewhere. Look at the picture on the right. There is almost no space behind him, but I left a gap of space in front of him. This is a cool way of suggesting movement. Also, notice the picture on the right has no fence in the backgound. It looks a little more real without the distractions.

Here's a fun project to try.... Imagine you're the family pet and go through their daily routine with a camera. Start by getting down at about the dog's eye level. Now do all of the shots from his point of view. Imagine all the things a dog might do durring the day. He has to get out of bed, take a drink, get some breakfast, bury a bone, find a bone, play in the yard, chase some birds and the list can go on almost forever. Dogs, being the loyal and loving creatures they are, will also follow people around the house. You could get some funny shots of the back of someone's feet as if you're a dog following them around the house. Maybe next he'll go back to bed and take a nap before the kids get home from school so he has plenty of energy to play! Remember this point of view idea when doing the same thing for other animals or people. When you take a bunch of photos that are going to be put together to tell a story, you are creating a Photo Essay. Sports magazines, news papers, and how-to books use this style of photography a lot. Take a look at some for ideas.

It's amazing how many things there are to take pictures of in the back yard. Let's start with some flowers. Flowers can be shot from a distance, or up close, it just depends on the look you're trying to get. Closeups are especially fun because you can catch the mist dripping off the plants, closeups of the pollen, and insects going to work in the flowers or on the branches. Talk to you parents about what kind of insects, or any other kind of creatures you should stay away from while shooting your back yard. As a matter of fact, you should talk to your parents about any of the information or projects in this book before doing them.

These flowers are called Daisies. They come in all kinds of colors and shades and love to be in front of a camera. Notice the detail in the center of these flowers. Insects are often attracted to the Pollen in center of the flower.

Another really cool looking flower is the Orchid. Orchids are a little bit harder to grow and are often inside greenhouses or grown indoors, but may be found outside in some places. They come in many varieties, sizes, shapes, and colors. The colors in Orchids are often very bright making them a lot of fun to shoot with the camera. If you do find these outside, Good job!

Roses are not only pretty flowers, but are also easy to find in most cases. A lot of people like to grow roses because they are hardy plants as well as looking nice. Roses attract lots of insects, especially bees. If you look at the bees really close, you can see them gathering clumps of pollen with their legs. One of the things you need to know about Roses is that they usually have thornes, Very Sharp ones, that cut you or poke you. Keep a safe distance from Rose bushes so you don't get hurt! They can even cut right through your clothes. Do Not get too close to bees, They will sting you if they get scared. Some kids are allergic to bee stings or have reactions to other insects. Check with your parents before approaching any insects just to be safe.

Notice the rose in the lower right corner has water or dew on part of the flower. You see this in the morning as the mist settles on the flowers. Other flowers have this happen as well. This water adds a nice effect to the picture. That's why you'll see it used a lot in magazines. Here's a cool trick, if your flowers don't have any water or dew on them, try spraying water on them with a spray bottle. This will give you that misty effect even on a dry day. Sometimes you can go out and check the flowers right after the sprinklers have turned off and you will see this effect, too. photographers use these tricks.

Insects are another cool thing to take pictures of in the back yard. You probably don't even realize how many little creepy crawlers and butterflies are in your back yard until you actually start paying attention. They're everywhere out there! In the lawn, on the plants, in the trees, on the ground, and just about anywhere else you can think of. Some insects are very pretty while others are a little scary looking. There's a whole world to explore!

Tiger Striped Swallow tail

Buck eye

Monarch Caterpillar

Monarch Butterflies

Tawny Emperor

Locust

Green Beatle

Praying Mantis

Birds are usually in the backyard as well. Birds can be a little bit of a challenge at first because they move so fast and often shy away from people. If you get too close, you'll usually scare them away. They're actually pretty smart animals and have a lot of personality, too. There are several ways to encourage birds to visit your backyard. Puting out a bird feeder or seeds, water, certain flowers and plants, and objects that shine are just a few of the ways to get birds to visit you. It will take a little practice to catch them in action, but you can do it. Since birds move so fast, here's a couple tips to help you get a good shot. Make sure you have enough light because you're going to need a fast shutter speed. Set your camera on sport mode if you have a dial with settings on it. keep your distance and use your zoom function instead of trying to get physically closer to the bird, they like to keep their distance. Did I mention that birds love fountains!

There's lots more out there, too!

Family and Friends... There are several ways of taking pictures of people. One of the ways to take pictures of people is Candid Shots. Candid meaning they either didn't know you were taking pictures of them, or they were just doing something else and not paying much attention to the camera. They are not posing, just being themselves. Candid photos of people can tell a story when you put them all together. Does this sound Familiar yet? When you put them together to tell a story it's a Photo Essay. This can be really fun for holidays and birthday parties. Here's some samples of Candid Photos...

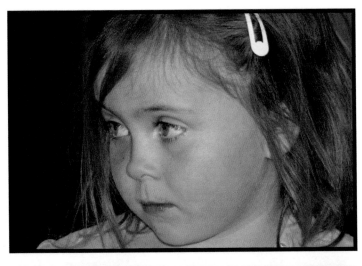

43

Posing for the camera is another way of shooting people. With posed shots, the people know they are being photographed and they try to look a certain way depending on what the photographer is trying to portray. Posed shots are used in portaits, commercials, and even family photos. Most of the time, the person posing is smiling, but you can have them do other expressions as well. The person (also called subject) can be sitting, standing, kneeling, or how ever else you'd like them to pose. Try to find the angles that really make the subject look good. Remember the tips for good lighting and the "shoulders back and chin up" routine to eliminate unwanted shadows.

Sometimes you may have to slightly change locations. If you're in the park and the sun is too bright, try having them stand under a tree. Try not to shoot towards the sun. For the most part, you want your back to the sun when shooting a posed type of shot. If the sun is so bright that it makes them squint, try moving slightly to the right or left. If a background is too cluttered or just doesn't look good, try zooming in closer on the person to get rid of some of that clutter.

Part of the trick to good portrait shots is picking a good background for the subject.If the person you are taking pictures of loves softball, it may be a good idea to use a baseball field or park to take pictures of them. Another thing you may want to consider is "props" The person that loves softball may want to dress in their uniform, and bring things like a bat, ball, or catcher's glove. When you add a nice background and a couple props, your picture will really tell a story about that person.

Props are not limited to baseball items or even sports. If a person enjoys animals, you may want to have them bring their dog or other pet. If a person likes nature, you may want a nice waterfall, trees, or something else that connects their interests with the picture you are taking. Costumes are cool for doing funny shots. Just about anything you can think of can be used as a prop. It all depends on your subject and what they are interested in or are trying to portray. Double check your props before you use them in the pictures. Get rid of any unwanted stickers or price tags on the items. You may also want to wipe the item down or clean it somehow. If you're not sure what kinds of props to use, ask the person you're going to take the picture of. Most people will appreciate the extra effort you're taking.

Family Poses

Individual Posers

Family Vacation Photos!

Now that you have become a photographer, it's time to have some fun with with those pictures. The first project is a Funny Card. Supplies needed for this project include a 4"x6" photo, an 8"x 10" piece of construction paper, paste (or glue), and some drawing materials such as crayons, pens, or pencils. * You can also add stickers, glitter, or anything else you think would make your card look great.

STEP ONE - Fold the construction paper in half. (from the long side)

STEP 2 - Pick out a photo to paste onto the front of the folded card. Once you have picked out the photo, paste it onto the front of the card. Try to center the photo into the middle of the card. After you have pasted to picture onto the paper, give the card some time to dry before going on to the next step. Drying time will vary, but paste usually dries much faster than glue.

Alex is doing a pretty good job of trying to glue the picture onto the front of the card here. The picture is centered on the card so he will have plenty of room for the next step. If at all possible, I suggest paste instead of glue because it dries faster and makes less of a mess when it comes time to clean up the area.

Notice how they are doing the projects outside. I just threw an old sheet over a table and placed all the supplies in the middle. I then put some plastic chairs around the table and had five kids playing at the same time. They interacted, laughed, and shared.

STEP 3 - Draw pictures around the edges of the photo that's pasted in the middle of the card to make a fun border. Along with the drawings you can also add stickers, glitter, or other things that will make your project stand out. The sky is the limit here, use your imagination!

Allison has just finished the outside of her first card. She decided to add a few butterfly stickers around the edges to give it some extra color.

On her card, she decided to make it flip up to open instead of making it open from the side. How the card opens depends on how you paste the picture on the front of it. Once you have pasted the picture and have created a border, flip the card open a couple times so you know if your card opens from the side or from the bottom.

STEP 4 - Just open the card and write something inside. The cards can be made for any occassion.

The next project will be an easy way to show off your photos... You're going to make a Picture Frame. You'll need the following items to complete this project.... construction paper, paste (or glue), something to draw with such as crayons, pencils, or markers, scissors (BE CAREFULL!) an 8"x 10" photograph, and something to hang the picture with such as string, twine, yarn, or ribbon. Never run or horseplay with scissors.

Peyton decided to use a picture taken in the Spring prior to writing this book. She did a pretty good job matching the color of the frame with the colors in the background of the picture, too.

STEP 1 - Pick out a photo and paste it into the center of the construction paper. let this picture dry before going onto the next step.

STEP 2 - Draw a frame or other fun picture around the photo.

STEP 3 - On the top of the picture frame, make a hole on the right and left side of the construction paper.

STEP 4 - Tie the string or yarn from one side to the other, but make sure the string is long enough to have a bow in it. This will make sure the picture will be able to hang by the string. Notice in the picture about how the string has plenty of room to hang from. You may need the scissors to cut the extra string off after you tie it on.

STEP 5 - Hang it up! This is another project you can add extras like glitter or stickers to.

Making a Puzzle out of your pictures... To make a puzzle, you'll need a large photograph (8"x 10") or larger, a marker or pencil, and a pair of scissors. Again, always be careful while using scissors.

STEP 1 - The first step is to pick out a large photo to make your puzzle with. Try using a photo that is at least 8"x 10". After you have decided which photo you would like to use, turn the photo over to the plain white side.

STEP 2 - Using a marker or pencil, draw some squiggles or other shapes that would make a good puzzle. Remember that you will be cutting these shapes out with scissors, so don't make the shapes too small to cut out. Parents or teachers working with younger children may want to draw the puzzle shapes on the back of the photos. Small children often do not understand their limits with finger dexterity and will draw shapes too difficult to cut out. The actual cutting out should be left to the kids as long as it's safe. On the next page is a sample of some shapes that can be used for creating a photo puzzle. It can even be traced onto the back of their picture with carbon paper, then gone back over with a marker before cutting.

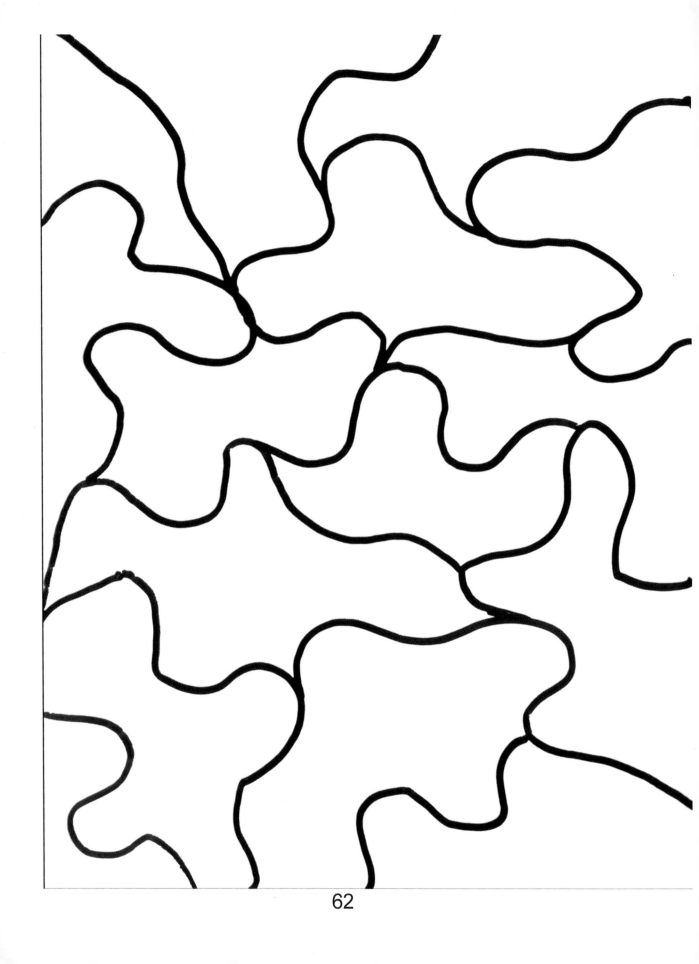

STEP 3 - While you are still looking at the back side of the photograph, cut along the lines you have created with the scissors. These are going to be the pieces of the puzzle. Remember not to cut the pieces to small, the puzzle will not come together correctly if the pieces are too small.

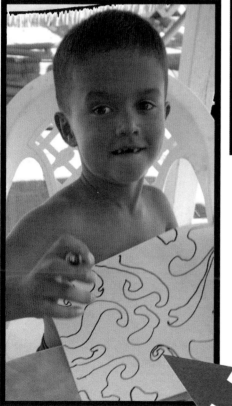

Allison, Alyssa, and Alex each have a different style for creating their puzzle pieces and they all look great! Some of the lines on the back of these photos may be too difficult to cut out with a pair of scissors. The swirl marked on Alex's photo is a pretty tough one to cut. In this case he may need to skip that curve while cutting out the pieces, but that's the good thing about doing the drawing on the back side of the puzzle, once It's turned over to the photo side you won't see the lines. If kids do draw a difficult shape, talk to them before they cut.

STEP 4 - Once all the shapes are cut out, turn the pieces over to the photo side and put them together! The pieces to the puzzle may be very small and easily lost. It's a good idea to have some small ziplock bags or sandwich bags to store the pieces in for rainy days.

Making Christmas Ornaments or other holiday decorations... You're going to need a few different colors of construction paper, something to draw with such as crayons, colored pencils, or markers, some small photos such as 4"x 6" or smaller, string or ribbon, and a pair of scissors. As with the other projects, be careful while using scissors. This book will use Christmas as an example, but decorations can be made for any holiday or occassion you'd like to celebrate.

STEP 1 - Cut some pieces of construction paper into interesting shapes such as bulbs, bells, tree, or other fun holiday shapes. Don't worry about the scraps, they may come in handy for the next project.

STEP 2 - Cut the photos into similar shapes as the construction paper, but make them a little smaller. The idea is to get them to fit into the pieces of construction paper.

STEP 3 - Once you have the pieces of construction paper and photos cut, paste the photos into the middle of the construction paper shapes.

STEP 4 - Add drawings, writing, stickers, glitter, or anything else you would like to help decorate your ornaments.

STEP 5 - Make a hole near the top / middle portion of the ornament.

STEP 6 - Tie a piece of string, ribbon, or yarn at the top of the ornament so it can be hung on the tree or other place that needs some decorating.

Making cool pages for your Scrapbook can be a lot of fun and there is no limit to the ideas you can come up with. Items you'll need to start your scrapbook... construction paper, photographs, scissors, squiggly scissors, crayons, pens, stickers, paste (or glue) and a scrapbook. There are many sizes and shapes for scrapbooks, but I'm using two different sizes. The large ones are for 8"x 10" photographs and the small scrapbooks are for 4"x 6" photographs. There is really no right or wrong way to make a scrapbook, but here's some pointers... Be careful with the scissors.

1) Make the photographs smaller than the scrapbook pages.

2) Cut fun shapes out of different colors of construction paper, use the shapes in front of, and behind the photos.

3) You can write different things on the pieces of paper.

4) Try the straight scissors and the squiggly scissors.

5) Add more fun to each page with glitter, stickers, or anything else you'd like to add. You may even want to try leaves, flowers, ribbons, pieces of cloth, or other items to add to the creative design.

6) Once you have the page all finished, place it into the scrapbook. You should be able to add lot more pages to the scrapbook.

One of the nice things about this project is that you can use the scraps cut out from all the other projects in the book. This way you don't have to waste any paper or other supplies.

Another nice thing is that there's no right or wrong way to scrapbook and there's almost no limits or set rules.

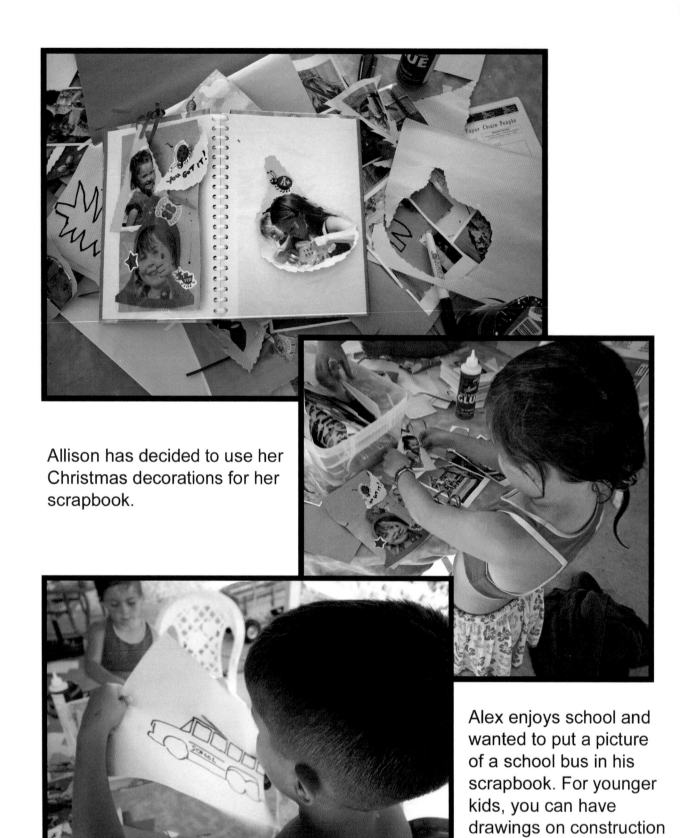

Allison has decided to use her Christmas decorations for her scrapbook.

Alex enjoys school and wanted to put a picture of a school bus in his scrapbook. For younger kids, you can have drawings on construction paper ready to cut.

Peyton loves using stickers and has used them in many of her projects. She's also really fast at doing her projects and became the teacher's aid. Some kids are faster than others so you may want to have other projects available.

More random shapes and cool stickers were used here.

Having multiple kids at the table also encourages sharing and exchanging of ideas. All four of the kids were talking, laughing, and coming up with ideas at this table.

This book has over 100 captivating photos with some of the information such as ISO, shutter speed, and aperture settings under each image. There will be a little dialog once in a while about a certain lens, filter, or technique, but most of the book is a chance to look at the images and decide what kind of composition you would like to experiment with on your on own. Incorporated in the collection is different lighting, color, and field of depth combinations so you can decide what kind of shots you'd like to play with. Above all else, if you enjoy animals and wild life, you'll probably love this book. It's geared towards people transitioning from a point and shoot to a DSLR camera, but is useful at all levels.

Scenic Photography Using Examples from the California Central Coast

A Visual Guide to the Central Coast and Digital Photography

This book is a visual guide to the California Central Coast through the use of vibrant, beautiful images. The photos are separated by location. Each location has a brief narrative that includes interesting features of that area and somtimes a hint or tip. Whether you're a photography or just love nature, you'll probably enjoy this book.

Publication Date: Jul 03 2008
ISBN/EAN13: 1438251114 / 9781438251110
Page Count: 72
Binding Type: US Trade Paper
Trim Size: 8" x 10"
Language: English

As well as having books for the younger audience, John Crippen also has books available for teens and adults. These books are digital photography field guides full of hints, tips, and examples great for the advance point and shoot or people transitioning to their first DSLR. They include helpful advice on purchasing a DSLR and essential equipement, too. They are available at many bookstores.

Cameras FOR KIDS!

A FREE LESSON PLAN can now be downloaded at the CamerasForKids.Info website. Teachers, parents, and others interested in early childhood education are encouraged to visit the website and check out the lesson plan. Hints and tips for optimizing time and getting the most of of this class are also included. The class does not require bringing in digital cameras or computers to save on expenses and keep the flow of the class moving well. The lesson plan is targeted for kids from 6 to 10 years of age, but may be appropriate for other ages as well. below is the link to the page with the article and plan..

http://www.camerasforkids.info/teachers.htm

CAMERAS FOR KIDS is more than just a book. On the CFK website, There's a variety of subjects for kids, parents, and teachers to get involved in. Along with all of the good information on photography, there's also articles on animals, nature, and green science. The website is designed to be a child enrichment resource center with the articles, tips, reviews, and much more. We are currently in the process of doing in class presentations and other community events, too. This book, along with other books have been donated to various libraries and school districts to help make this information available to kids everywhere. If this content is not available in your local libraries, districts, or bookstores, you may want to let them know about the project.

THANK YOU to the educational and family communities that have helped make this program possible! Thank you for all of the positive feedback as well. As the program continues to grow and expand, we would love to get as much feedback as possible to make sure that we're moving in a positive direction. Please feel free to contact us at our Website, Blog, or Email. We also have pages on social networks such as Facebook and Myspace. For the little one's, don't forget to visit Herbie's Hints!

Excerpts from the critics...

"Camera's for Kids is well written and organized. This book takes the mystery out of taking good pictures." - **Readers Favorites, Hawesville, KY USA**

"In an age when more and more parents tend to complain about the sedentary, video game-obsessed culture in which their children are being raised, Cameras For Kids provides a wide assortment of healthy alternatives, encouraging children not only to engage their minds - but also their bodies - in the active exploration of the world around them." - **Apex Reviews, Durham, NC USA**

"I love this book and here's why: 1. Easy to read 2. Easy to understand. 3. Easy to do projects. 4. The kids WANT to do the projects. 5.The kids are learning about photography. 6. I'm learning about photography!! 7. FAMILY TIME FUN!!! If you pick up a copy for yourself, pick up an extra for gifts, the classroom, or your Sunday school class. I wish Mr. Crippen would write a book that would make homework or piano lessons as fun!!" - **Kelli Stapleton of Birth Stories on Demand**

"Cameras for Kids will hopefully serve as a guide to photography and artistic expression for the little photographer / artist". - **Stan Ashbrook, PSA Journal (Photographers Society of America)**

"What a wonderful book! It is sure to spark our students' interest." - **Cris L. Smith, District Librarian for the Atascadero Unified School District, in Atascadero, California**

"I'm sure students will enjoy and learn from this book for years to come." - **Linda Coburn, Library Tech, San Gabriel Elementary**

Made in the USA
San Bernardino, CA
04 October 2014